From Pots to Plastics

FROM POTS TO PLASTICS

Written and illustrated by ANNE JOLLIFFE

History adviser PETER CARPENTER
(Cambridge Institute of Education)

HAWTHORN BOOKS, INC.   *Publishers   New York*

J
600
J

Long ago, in the OLD STONE AGE,
man hunted for his food
and made his home in caves and other
rough shelters.

To protect himself from cold
and from wild animals
he learned how to use
FIRE.

When he began to
grow crops for food,
man built villages
near the fields.

Bricks were made
of mud and
pots of clay.

These were left to
dry in the sun
or BAKED hard
beside the fire.

By grinding corn
FLOUR was made.

With the DOUGH
made by mixing flour
and water, BREAD
was baked in brick
OVENS.

When something is COOKED in this
way an important change takes place.

This is called a CHEMICAL CHANGE,
and cooking can be thought of as
the beginning of CHEMISTRY.

It was found
that better bricks
and pots could
be made by
baking them in
special ovens
called
KILNS.

In very hot FURNACES
man MELTED certain
kinds of rock to get
METALS.

At first these metals
were beaten into
shape to make tools
and weapons.

Later man learned
how to CAST metals.

To get the metals he
needed man became
a miner, digging into
the ground for copper,
silver, lead and tin.

By mixing together
different metals new
hard ALLOYS were made.

11

The best of these alloys was B R O N Z E,
which is made by mixing together copper
and tin.

Near great rivers some of the Stone Age
villages grew into
Bronze Age Cities.

Bronze was very expensive. Only kings of rich cities could afford to arm their soldiers with bronze weapons.

In time it was found that
better and cheaper weapons
could be made from IRON,
which was more plentiful.

BARBARIAN invaders with
iron weapons destroyed
the Bronze Age cities.

The IRON AGE began.

The country we know as Greece was conquered by
people who used iron weapons.

They sailed the seas in order to trade.

From distant lands they brought
home many new IDEAS and built a
great civilization of their own.

Many important discoveries were made
and written down.

This was the beginning of true SCIENCE.

The ideas of
the Greeks spread
to many lands.

17

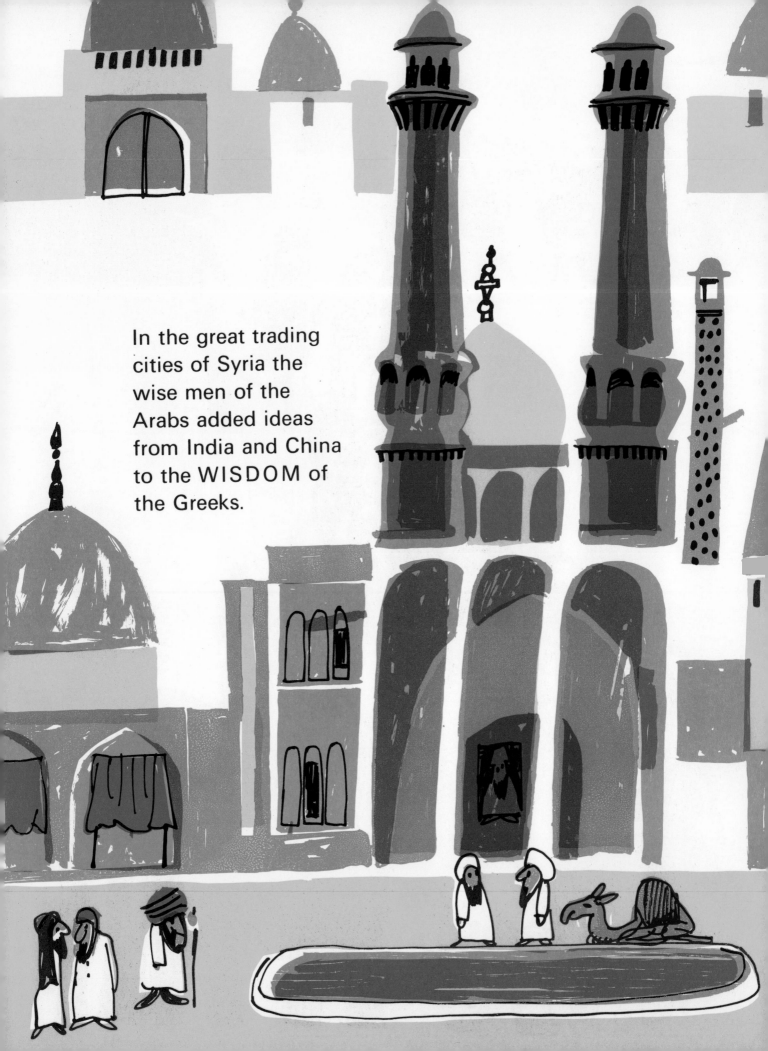

In the great trading cities of Syria the wise men of the Arabs added ideas from India and China to the WISDOM of the Greeks.

But often MAGIC and MYSTERY were mixed up with scientific ideas.

With magic spells and powders
the ALCHEMISTS worked in their LABORATORIES.

One of the things they were trying to do was to turn ordinary metals into gold.

Of course they could not make gold,
but while they were trying to do so
they discovered many useful
CHEMICALS.

GLASS BLOWERS made bottles and flasks
for the alchemists to use in their EXPERIMENTS.

For many years
GUNPOWDER had been
used in China to make
fireworks.

The alchemists of the
MIDDLE AGES also
discovered how to make
gunpowder.

The INVENTION of gunpowder
brought about many changes.

Now even harder metals were
needed to make the huge guns
used in warfare.

Eventually
BLAST FURNACES
were built to make
iron into
STEEL.

Coal was mined as a FUEL
for the new furnaces.

But coal mines were full
of dangerous GASES.

By studying these gases, man discovered OXYGEN. The oxygen in the air we breathe helps to keep us alive.

He also found that our bodies behave as fire does, burning up food and oxygen to make HEAT and ENERGY.

Alchemy had become the modern science of chemistry.

Chemists discovered that everything in the world is made up of tiny PARTICLES, called ATOMS.

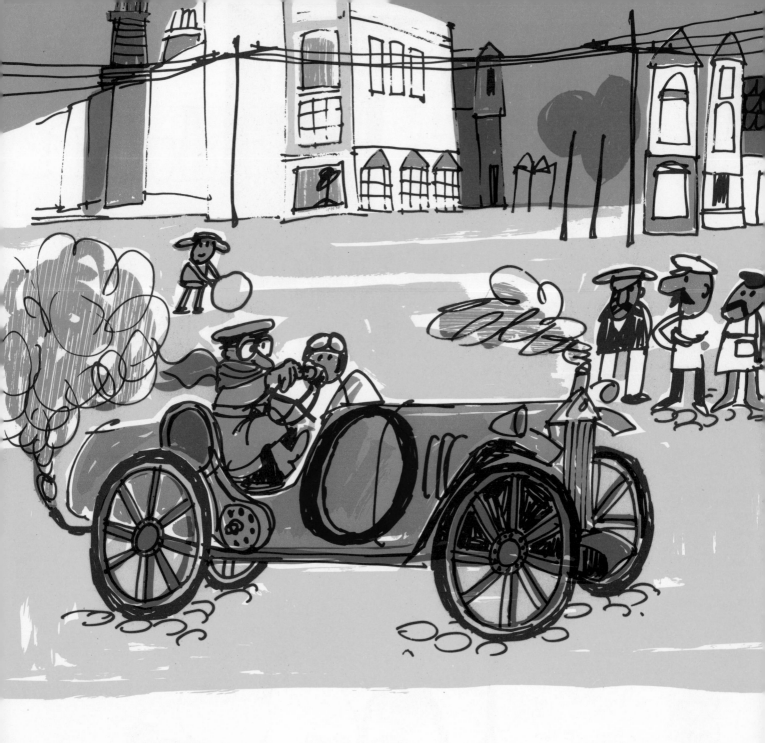

Scientists next discovered how these atoms are arranged,
and from this knowledge they were able to make new
man-made things, such as
ARTIFICIAL RUBBER.

Man can also make MATERIALS
that have never
been seen before,
such as PLASTICS.

He can improve his health with VITAMIN tablets
and fight disease with DRUGS, such as
PENICILLIN.

In the future, with all kinds of new
materials, man will be able to do
even more wonderful things.

Perhaps he will be able
to fly right away
from the earth and
make his home on other
PLANETS.

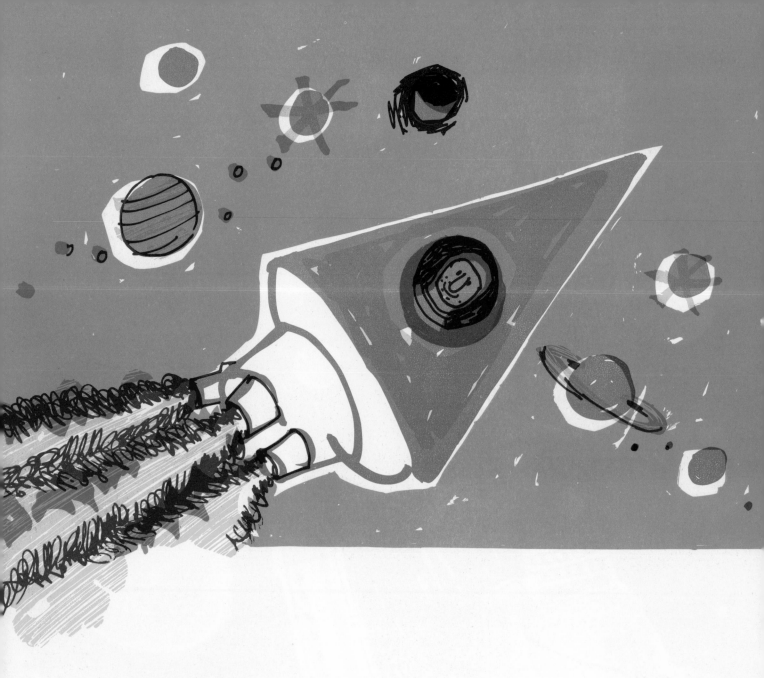

We know now that it is not
by magic, but by using his
KNOWLEDGE and INGENUITY,
that man can build a better world.

Date Due

DEC 3 '68					
FEB 20 '69					
MAY 12 '69					
OC 2 1 '70					
DEC 2 1 '79					
DEC 1 2 1990					

PRINTED IN U.S.A.　　CAT. NO. 23231